Light And Dark

A Collection of Sonnets

Ronald Slomba

BookLeaf Publishing

India | USA | UK

Made with ❤ on the BookLeaf Publishing Platform
www.bookleafpub.in
www.bookleafpub.com

Dedication

I'd like to dedicate this to anyone who has ever picked
me up when I've fallen down

Preface

This is a collection of sonnets mostly Shakespearean in
rhyme scheme
I'm beginning to tinker with other forms of sonnets
Feeling less weary to stray from the path the more
comfortable I am getting with writing
Mostly I like to express myself by putting my feelings
onto the page

Acknowledgements

I'd like to acknowledge and thank Bookleaf Publishing
and their 21 days poem a day challenge
#TheWriteAngle Writing Challenge

1. Hope

Hope is for summers
Sowed by the spring
Thunderous showers
Blooms they shall bring

When the storm fades
The sun shall appear
Thought hidden by shades
The light remains near

If one looks they will find
Hope isn't hidden
Peer into the mind
One will hear if they listen

In order to start just believe and begin
Abundant as the sky, one needs simply to breathe it in

2. Lunaris

Her light may be borrowed
Lit up against a world of black
Fading into tomorrow sorrowed
But she'll never turn her back

Her face glows so warm
With a side you'll never know
Every night she is born
Or so it looks but doesn't show

Above a yearning world that's turning
She won't allow herself to walk away
Her face laid bare laid burning
She presses onward anyway

Some days she's early, some nights she's late
Waxing or waning, she can't escape her fate

3. The Tangled Path

I used to fight for my life alone
Out there in my wilderness
Howling at the moon regardless
At least it was my own

Still much remains left unknown
As light fades to darkness
Here the sky is starless
At least we're not alone

No hovel left for the shame
What was once wild now lies tame

Mourning for helping hands mangled
Disturbed I wake in my perilous plight
Further every night I sink into the blight
Weaving forward the path ahead is tangled

4. Tides

Tonight I lie awake something like the night before
Waiting for another full moon that I'll never see
Waiting for my light to return once more
Tonight the tide is rising all around me

Sink or swim in this cold cold world
A single light goes dim and my world enshrouds in
darkness
Frigid in its wake the torrents whirled
Crashing on the rocks I'm thankful for their hardness

I envy how they can stand against the ocean
The tide draws to my light scatters it across the strand
I pray for strength the world breaks me open
Hardship forges treasures from the sand

Tides will come, tides will go
I'll stand ready for the ebb and flow

5. Blackout

I am not victimless
No stranger to sin
Desires of the flesh
Things I've done to win

I lay no claim to pity
Mark me for my crimes
Every mistake made gritty
Carved into the times

A folly to boast of loss
Lessons learned the most
The taste of bitter dross
Stings down to the ghost

Pain me in my poison that my stain may fade
Erasure of the memoires delirium pervade

6. Grief

Whilst parting is such sweet sorrow
Know that I'll see you on the morrow
When the storm parts and the sky is calm
My heart finds comfort in a psalm

At these times I remember life's a choice
And though I know you'd rather I rejoice
I know not where I'm fueled to go
Absorbed in memories from long ago

Grief is like a bullet hole that just won't heal
Your gone now I'm not whole, this can't be real
Like drops of rain formed from the storm
These tears rain down without reform

Our time here after all is not so long
So in a psalm I find the faith to be strong

Psalm 23:4

Yea, though I walk through the valley of the shadow of
death

I'll fear no evil: for thou art with me

Reflection

They may be gone but not forgotten

Yea, though this time on earth is fleeting

Cherish there memories in your heart, for they are not
defeating

Find solace in the harsh truth

This feeling it becomes common

7. Twinkling

You will always be so beautiful
Like every twinkle in the sky
This much is indisputable
Twinkling even as we say goodbye

How I wonder lost in black
Can we again begin
Light shines through as I begin to crack
I can't let what I wonder win

Break me down until I'm new
Until what was left is gone
Betrayed by my thoughts for you
The pain of moving on

You brought me up so high with a diamond
Now I'll build myself back up as an island

8. Perception

Dealings with death are simple
If perception is so kind
Illuminating the way forward
A fragrant sight even to the blind

And if I give into despair the enemy shall win
"Nothing will change no matter the dismay"
Or "What can be done tomorrow better than today"
Struggles in this reality need not begin

Death is trivial if you believe it conquered
If once then again he will rise anew
As it is written in the word
Death is trivial if you believe it true

His house has many rooms for those who love
As they've so been prepared up above

9. Class C

I once flew so high above
Soaring free as any dove
Life's pace a gentle breeze
Your love put me at ease

Never conceiving a storm so strong
In its wake you would be moving on
Struck with lightning and I'm sinking
Shocked the spark in me is leaving

Leering eyes begin to theory
What was I even to you really

Did you ever really want love
When they push tell them to shove
It's none of their concern
For I was always yours to burn

10. Sometimes

You're gonna be alright
Everything's gonna be okay
You'll make it through this fight
All that pains gonna wash away

As many times as it may take
Fall and know you'll make it through
Cuz those helping hands won't ever break
They'll always be there to catch you

When nothing else will soothe
Let it out because you know the truth

It won't turn down your shine
When those clouds go awry
Stand tall without resign
Because even sunflowers cry
...Sometimes

11. Mustard Story

Love begins as a mustard seed
A picnic basket on a sunny beach
A sandwich made just right and some cold mead
Water it well and it will begin to reach

Beginning small and seemingly insignificant
Before long it becomes the tallest of the trees
Before long it becomes magnificent
More beautiful than one foresees

Love's growth is not bound by a lifetime
Love's patience knows no duration
Marriage is the start of your climb
Eternity is the destination

Now greater than the sum of your parts combined
May you both grow together forever entwined

12. Wasted Gifts

Heart of an artist
Innovator of the mind
I know I'm not the sharpest
Sometimes I even feel blind

Flare for the dramatic
Perhaps I chose this trauma
Empathic cinematic
I wrote my own drama

Born too soon or too late
This can't be my time
I pray for knowledge of my fate
I repent because I did the crime

Give first to be given
Forgive first to be forgiven

13. Nakedness

Asking myself questions like why does this always
happen to me
You'll come back I won't be ready then you'll blame it on
me
More times now than three
Didn't think I'd ever do this again when I bent my knee
They sure don't know what they want but its not me
Rip my heart out watch myself bleed
Let them see me bleed, let them see me for me
See me bare see me naked
There's only one of you but you've got so many
faces
It's no wonder its so hard for you to face it
You tell me your jumping off the train
Leaving me behind
I won't cut off my family
So you're off this is goodbye
So I'll lick my wounds as you turn your back
Howl to the moon and go back to the pack

14. Misery

Misery loves company
Like a murder of crows
Misery flocks to the unlovely
It oozes and it grows

Those hearts empty of forgiveness
They rumble and they grown
Loving with such stiffness
Uncontent with what they've sown

Counsel becomes stone
Spite turns perception black
Blessed be the crone
That lets compassion act

Pray thee freedom of weights placed upon thine self
For else thy mind becomes prison, shackles to one's
health

15. This October

October is for pumpkins and cider
Notaries giving their vouch
October is for the witch and the spider
Deciding who keeps which couch

October is for Vampires and Coffins
Driving U-hauls to storage lockers
October is for ghouls and goblins
Divvying up shared coffers

October is for the living to pay respect to the dead
For painted faces and costumes to trick for treats
This October has days of joy mixed with days of dread
Some days will be sour and some days will be for sweets

This October we'll remember until our days are through
This October I"ll sign the papers separating me from you

16. Denial

Two swings
White picket fence
Darlin I need two things
What's your two cents

Understanding and forgiveness
Let's make amends
Resonance without recompense
Broken before we bent

I ask you if you need more time to think
Your expression as if I said something strange
You answer before I can even blink
Nothing is ever going to change

My greatest lesson didn't happen by mistake
The grass always looks greener when its fake

17. Winter Eternal

My heart is a blade of grass that longs for the first spring
rain
Quivering 'til it stops, the cold creeps in to cause it pain
Beats stop every winter waiting to sprout anew
Beckoned only by the spring that brings its first drop of
dew

Berated by frost 'til it sunders
Weathering the storm
A hibernation 'til spring thunders
Biding though its torn

Then blooming in a rush
Let our spring seep in
As the sprout longs for rain I long simply for your touch
Let our love begin

As the seed should not bloom if spring should detour
My heart is still without your warmth, Winter reigns
eternal more

18. Cuddles

Have I told you that I love you
That you're the only one
If I make one promise these words are true
I'll hold onto you until the world is done

So let me sweep you off you're feet
Take off with you into the setting sun
Where we can rewind and repeat
Our love has only just begun

Every day with you is a blessing
As the miracle of life itself
Would be a curse without your caressing
Your cuddles keep me in good health

Cuddles for anything whatever the weather
Perfect for training me and keeping me forever

19. Blessed Rain

Blessed be thy rain that fall upon thine face
To form the rivers, neigh the ocean
Rain that seems magnetic to your grace
Rain that's drawn to you as I may seem a silly notion

Rain that echoes my passion and makes the rivers flow
Rain flowing hither or thither wherever you should stroll
Waterfalls from the heavens would surely start to show
Drawn to their lost angel, downward they shall roll

Blessed was I the day you fell from the sky
The day I pledged myself to thee
To always remain with you standing by
To show you the true meaning of chivalry

Your grace has my heart melting skipping every beat
Warm palpitations to hot arrhythmia everytime we meet

20. Brighter Art

There's this something that happens whenever I'm
around you
This feeling that you make me feel
It's getting hard to tell that I'm not dreaming when my
arms surround you
Could this actually be real

I've been hoping wishing waiting
My whole life it seems
What once was the dullest painting
Now oh how it gleams

For every color is brighter here in your shade
Every canvas a piece of art
No signs tell of even the slightest of fade
The same to tell of my heart

An ever flowing chalice overflowing with ectasy
Words cannot describe just how happy you make me

21. Tenure

Tenure in my heart
You stole my heart for ten years
Loved you like an art
We worked on it for ten years

How did we get here
Threw me away like I was garbage
Left me broken hearted
Girly I was only getting started

Now that my life's a blank canvas
I'll paint my own new story
I'll start it over build myself a new campus
Off in safer territory

I never imagined this in my worst dreams
I guess fairy tales really are just make believe